The Shadow of Poverty

DIALOG JOURNALISM®: PUTTING INTO CONTEXT
GENERATIONAL POVERTY, STIGMA
AND HEALTH OUTCOMES

CHRISTINE MARIE NIELSEN

ISBN: 979-8-58-442179-3

Some names, characters and places may have been changed for privacy purposes.

Book design by GoOnWrite and Geodialog Media publishing.

Printed by Amazon, in the United States of America.

First printing edition 2020.

www.geodialogmedia.com

TABLE OF CONTENTS

Acknowledgements

Despite current difficulties, I thank my parents for giving me a reason to revisit my childhood home of Milwaukee, but this time with new eyes to see its fertile landscape for improvement. Thank you also to award-winning writers Michael McColly and Steve Bogira who gave me valuable insights as I began this journey.

Preface

I have a dark shadow on the gum tissue under my top lip. It's not obvious to everyone, but I know it's there.

The discoloration speaks of an injury that occurred amidst a childhood of poverty and an inability to completely eliminate poverty's effects on my life.

And just as a city bears a history, the body bears a history as well. In time, I've come to learn that my fate, and the fate of the city where I grew up - Milwaukee, which is one of the poorest and most segregated cities in the U.S. - are closely intertwined.

Milwaukee was in the national news a lot in 2020 because of the killing of people of color by police, nonviolent and violent demonstrations, high covid rates and multiple mass shootings. It's difficult to truly understand the dynamics at play in the city though, without taking a deep dive to put it all into context.

In the creation of this piece, I had conversations and dug through newspaper clippings and historical documents in an attempt to discover the bigger picture of the city for myself and others. I pulled back the curtain, in a sense, discovering how generational poverty has impacted my life and how it continues to impact my hometown.

The piece was used as a launchpad for an online Dialog Journalism® event from Geodialog Media LLC (geodialogmedia.com). Geodialog Media's Dialog

Journalism® involves creating a solution-focused dissemination of news that integrates traditional international editorial content and an online social media forum in an effort to resolve global issues. Geodialog Media provides an Internet news portal featuring links to news stories and articles about current events and includes a website featuring articles and RSS feeds, micro blogging feeds, and video in the field of current events.

Introduction

From what I've seen and heard, an effective first step in eliminating the cycle of poverty is to bring into the light current conditions and their results on individuals impacted by those conditions. The second step is to form human relationships that can bridge the gaps between those without resources and those with resources.

The World Health Organization Charter states that "health is a state of complete physical, mental and social well-being and not merely the absence of disease or infirmity." The WHO estimates that only about 10 percent to 15 percent of health is determined by care as social circumstances, behaviors, and environment decide the rest.

For those who live in a cocoon because of their race, gender, or educational opportunities, it's easy to ignore groups that are left behind, or shun them altogether because of the urge to dwell in a sense of safety from the world's ills.

I lived in such a cocoon separated from the financial insecurities of my parents - that is, until I couldn't distance myself anymore. Now I'm trying to explore the conditions of Milwaukee, its people who are often underinsured and undertreated in terms of health, and the poor treatment I've seen with my mother and myself.

As in many sections of the U.S. and large rust belt cities, the problems in Milwaukee are systemic, and a large range of people suffer because of ill-conceived policies and a government that has ignored a large number of the city's inhabitants. Those who are affected the most have little agency to alter their situations; therefore poverty passes from generation to generation.

Frustration about this lack of agency boiled to the surface as homicides headed toward 200 in the Milwaukee area in 2020, fatal shootings by police grew, Covid-19 took a heavy toll - especially on African-Americans - with around half of all deaths from the virus hitting that community. Further, political differences mounted as the presidential election resulted in a state recount request by President Donald Trump, with Wisconsin considered a key battleground state in the election.

The pressure had also been building for some time because of less publicized reasons. This lack of agency was illustrated, for example, when it was announced that in December of 2018 the YMCA that served Milwaukee's African-American community for years was to be downsized. The weightlifting center and workout area would be cut out of the Parklawn YMCA at 46th and Congress in Milwaukee's inner city, an area which is highly populated by African Americans. In fact, about 90 percent of African-Americans in the Milwaukee area live in the City of Milwaukee. YMCA directors told the local media that the changes would allow the facility to offer more programs, including a "Silver Sneakers" exercise program for seniors in conjunction with insurance companies.[6061]

After hearing the plans for the closure, local Alderman Khalif Rainey issued a statement, saying, in part, "the proposed changes equate to a lack of recreational and health-related opportunities for that area. The results are too many young men with not enough to do, leading to increased bad behavior and even worse public health outcomes. When I say even worse, I'm referring to the fact that Parklawn is located in zip code, 53216, where more than 52 percent of its residents are obese which is among the highest obesity rates in the city of Milwaukee." He added that "the activities and facilities currently available to youth at the Parklawn YMCA have been a refuge for me, my neighbors, and the community as a whole. And with so many young people and families not having the means to travel to other YMCA branches as the organization has suggested, I request it changes course on the planned cuts…"[62]

Most of those cuts did take place as planned, serving as one of the many illustrations of how people who are already struggling through poverty, addictions, chronic health problems, and unsafe and often polluted environments are sometimes willfully neglected.

When I moved to Chicago in 1996 I worked as a financial reporter for Knight-Ridder Financial and later Dow Jones Newswires. I also did work for a handful of startups and even had a stint as an equity analyst in training until I eventually started my own LLC in 2012 that focuses on using dialogic-based journalism to support democracy and solve global issues. I didn't anticipate, however, that I'd ever have to return to the Milwaukee area and face economic challenges on behalf of my mother and myself, and I've suffered because of being on the outside of a media industry power center that dictates information flow.

>**Chapter 1: A Childhood Of Poverty**

What I've come to understand is that poverty itself is so ensnaring because it is both a trigger and an outcome. Factors such as family history, access to resources, chronic stress and health problems can lock in poverty conditions for multiple generations. The long-term impacts can have health ramifications, impact family structures and block social and economic mobility.

What is poverty? In 2018, the federal "poverty line" in 2018 for a family of four (two adults and two kids) was about $25,100.[1]

As of 2016, when the poverty line was $24,300,[2] government health care programs covered about 40 percent of kids. It's estimated that at least twice the poverty level figure would be needed to meet all of a family's needs.

What might this look like for a child? If a child were to live below the poverty line, he or she would be less likely to have parents who work at least part of the time. He would be likely to have parents that have less than a high school degree. He would be likely to live with one parent or another relative. He would be more likely to have moved in the last 12 months and would be more likely to be living in a rented home versus a house that belongs to the family.[3]

However, often children don't know they are technically living in poverty." One of my earliest memories involves me being in a little pink snowsuit and having to slide down the big slickly iced hill in front of our house to go to a waiting cab on the street. "Alright, you next," I remember the cab driver yelling to my mother. He caught us when we reached the sidewalk below. I had come down with a terrible cough and my mother was trying to get me to the doctor.

I was a child of the '70s, and during most of my childhood we lived at a duplex rental unit in the 600 block of South 60th Street in Milwaukee. The flat was in an area where most of the houses were built before 1939, and the majority of folks had attained a high school education, at best. Almost half of the households in the area were, and still are, occupied by people renting.[30]

We always wore socks or shoes indoors, as we couldn't afford carpeting and the landlord wasn't supplying any. And much to my embarrassment as a child, we had only a black and white television set, while all of the other kids' families had a color set.

My best friend for much of the time we were living there was a little American-Indian girl. One day, she and her family were just gone. My mother told me they had left in the night. To this day I wonder what happened.

The 60th Street address rolled off the tongue, and I would say it in a sing-songy way when I was a child. We would wait for my dad's $112 child support check to arrive every month to do the grocery shopping. Because we had no car, we would walk to the corner grocery store[31] down the street from the park. I understand now we were living in what was at that time a food desert, with that store being the only option.[32] Frequently, we would end up throwing away bread we had bought because it tasted like the smell of cigarettes. (The cashier at the store was a heavy smoker.) There were also times when we got home and realized some of the food we had bought was expired.

When I was 12, we moved to another rental spot in the same zip code, closer to the area where my mom grew up. My brother, 13 years older and the product of my mom's first marriage, was already living at the address and had been recently divorced by his wife. My mom told me we'd moved to help my brother out.

In the area where we lived, 20.4 percent of children ages six to 11 years old currently live in poverty. I'm not exactly sure what the poverty rate among that age group was when I was a kid, but my guess is it may have been slightly lower. There was a jump in unemployment in the 2000s as Wisconsin saw two recessions.

I've done the math, and roughly with what my mother made and the check from child support, my mother couldn't have taken in more than $1,000 a month after taxes.

There were many times when it was just my mother and me, and she had to figure out how to take care of the both of us. Now it is up to me to try to take care of her needs. Doing so isn't always easy, or pretty.

Because of her economic and social situation, my mother has had a difficult life and intermittent rounds of health care.

As my mother ages, she professes "I am low income" to medical staff during the intake process at hospitals and clinics. I shudder every time she does it. I know it means she's shifting the medical staff's focus to a different mindset, and possibly a different level of care. She's had a long life of identifying herself in this way.

It hasn't been easy to obtain help, either. While it's common to hear tales of individuals who went to see lawyers with their elderly parents to get their affairs in order and ended up having to "spend down" their parents' assets to make them eligible to receive financial help,[5] my mother sees it in a different light. Though eligible, my mother for many years refused to accept Title 19, a federal program which would potentially take care of expenses such as assisted living costs or the cost of a nursing home.

What this has meant is more pressure on me, caring for the mother whom I love while I also work to support myself. The potential for a bleak future for myself makes me feel afraid, and I'm not alone with this fear among single middle-aged women in the U.S.

Predominantly single women who care for their elderly parents are over twice as likely to live in poverty compared to non-caregivers when they get older, according to research published by Rice University.[6] Poverty is a quicksand that's often difficult to escape. The more poverty makes you squirm, the deeper you sink.

My mother's decision to reject the financial help has left me tallying the potential costs of everything, and fearing potential pitfalls.

My mom was born in the summer of 1933. Her family had two sons and three daughters and suffered through the Depression. According to a University of Wisconsin, Milwaukee narrative,[4] by 1932 there were over 2,800 children in

Milwaukee that could be characterized as malnourished, and within a three-year span there were more than double that amount.

While socialists were in control in Milwaukee in the early '30s, the 1932 election brought Democrat Franklin D. Roosevelt to the presidency and handed his party control of the Congress. Roosevelt was president for much of my mother's childhood, and through the hardest of times of The Depression.

One child - my aunt - was closest to my grandparents and as an adult inherited the family home and the majority of its contents. My mother at one point told me she wanted to marry at a young age so she could "get away" from her family home. In the end, she never finished high school, and did leave her family home to marry.

My father was a U.S. Postal worker for 42 years. It was a good job by the blue-collar town of Milwaukee's standards - full benefits, a government job. In 1969, my dad married my mom, who at the time was working as the head cashier at the suburb of Milwaukee West Allis Hospital.

My father - who was my mom's second husband - divorced my mother in the 1970s, a time when child support was often given minimal focus in divorce situations. The child support collection system wasn't officially set up until 1975, when the U.S. government created Section IV-D of the Social Security Act.

Despite my parents' divorce when I was two, my father did dutifully participate in the school carpool, pay for a Lutheran grade school and high school education, and come to family vacations and dinners.

Being the "poor" kid at the Lutheran schools wasn't always a good look for me, however.

I can remember how one of the first boys I dated in high school (who had attended another private school in the area) broke up with me after a short romance. He asked if I had ever seen the movie *Pretty in Pink*. Confused by the reference, I asked him why. He was quick to tell me about the defined worlds of the rich, popular male character in the movie, and the working class girl lead. I may have been participating in one world, but some people obviously didn't see me as "one of them."

I had a similar experience when I was a young reporter working in Chicago and appearing at a Chicago Board of Trade press event as a representative of the *Wall Street Journal*. By that time, however, I had learned to blend in.

President George W. Bush was visiting the trading floor, and there was an event held later in the day for reporters. Perhaps still on a high from getting a warm greeting on the floor, Bush turned to the group of reporters standing on the sidelines - including myself and a young woman from a regional newspaper. He heartily shook our hands. The young woman turned to me. "These people would never even look at someone like me if I wasn't here for the paper," she said.

Following up on these recollections as I researched the stigma attached to generational poverty, I called Giridhar Mallya, the Public Health Physician and Senior Policy Advisor at philanthropy Robert Wood Johnson Foundation. Mallya told me that income inequity related to kids appears to be widening, and in the last

10 years, only people at the upper income strata have benefitted when the economy saw improvements. He noted that large differences in income make it hard for groups to interact. The situation "pulls at the social fabric," he said. Ultimately, it brings up the topic of "othering" he said, where a single person or group is thought of as an outsider because of their economic status, ethnicity, race, sex, disability, religion or sexual orientation.

The concept of "othering" is said to be rooted in the work of cultural theorist Edward W. Said. The work of Said did not come recently, but the word "othering" has been in the news as of late, as it's been used in conjunction with concerns about migrants entering the country.[20] Also in the news has been how in the U.S. the economic divides among existing citizens are quickly widening across income groups, geography, race and education.

One thing having experienced poverty does do, is it allows one to empathize with others who have been through similar trying conditions.

A customer service job at the local newspaper was a way for my mom to keep us all going and pay the bills. Eventually I would work at this newspaper as a young reporter, and eat lunches with my mom.

During one of my mom's final years at the newspaper she received a copy of a letter one customer had sent to the main office of the paper. "This woman touched me with her kindness after I told her that my son had brain cancer," the letter read. "She told me not to worry about the unpaid bill, but take care of my son instead."

The letter sits in a frame close to the tattered recliner where my mom now spends most of her days. I believe my mother may have paid the bill for that woman at that time to try to make things easier for her. This was despite my mother's own tight budget.

I'm standing in a long line at the Froedtert Hospital in Milwaukee's patient financial services office and I'm wondering how I ever got here, not necessarily how I got to this physical space, but how I arrived at this point in my life.

On this particular day, I'm trying to sort out why my $33-a-month payment plan at the hospital was canceled, even though I had faithfully been making the required payments before the due date each month. A year before, a woman at the financial services office had told me in a soft voice that as long as I paid the minimum due each month, any additional charges I incurred for my care within the Froedtert health care system - primary care or otherwise - could be added to the balance. The payments could be spread out over time, and the amount of the payments would remain the same.

The average credit score of someone with medical debt is 560. How do you get into medical debt? You get sick at a time that you don't have the depth of medical insurance or financial resources to cover the bills. It's estimated one in six individuals in the U.S. has derogatory marks on their credit reports for past-due medical expenses. And according to the Kaiser Family Foundation, medical bills were the main catalyst for over a million adults filing for bankruptcy in 2015.

What does a credit score below 600 mean? It means you would not be accepted on most credit card applications, be approved for a rental unit, for mortgages or for car loans. Medical bills create more debt as individuals cut corners or have to borrow, and this creates more problems.

The long-term effects of generational poverty have been identified by the Chronic Poverty Research Centre as poor nutrition, insufficient health care and education and lack of assets and a lack of opportunity that impact multiple generations.

Medical debt mushrooms into more debt. And skimping on things like dental cleanings and regular checkups sometimes results in more costly problems down the line and more serious medical conditions.

Despite knowledge of predatory lending practices, at one point I even took out a payday loan to pay a looming bill. The result was that even after I paid off that loan and its 120 percent interest (low, considering the national average rate for a payday loan is 400 percent), the lender kept taking money out of my bank account. The only thing that stopped them from doing so was when a Wells Fargo banker sat down with me in his office, closed the account and helped me to file a fraud report with the bank. I had to document everything very carefully and get an agreement in writing that the payday loan company would stop taking money out. Having someone's name at the payday loan company and holding them accountable seemed to be key.

It does tend to be the most financially vulnerable who utilize payday loans. Statistics show that as of 2018, people who have incomes of between $15,000 and $25,000 are most likely to take out payday loans. People who rent their homes are also twice as likely to use payday loans. And while I only took out one payday loan, using this type of credit often starts a cycle of signing on the dotted line on a second or third payday loan just to make the payments on the first payday loan. According to a CNBC survey, around 11 percent of the U.S. population utilized payday loans in 2017 and 2018.

But the stealthy account moves weren't only happening on the part of the payday loan company. When we were looking at my bank accounts, we realized someone at Wells Fargo had opened a savings account on my behalf without my permission. I had been incurring fees from that account without my knowledge.

When I was growing up, my father spoke of wealth as if it were some sort of magic. "Money is no object," my dad would murmur when a home improvement show would portray someone redoing their home with luxury materials. But for us, "beggars can't be choosers," he would say. The underlying message being we were beggars.

Now I have a new sense of the stigma associated with poverty, and how difficult it is to see what lies beyond the barriers of poverty.

When I first moved to Chicago, it was like arriving in Oz. So many possibilities. So much potential. I was young and enthusiastic. Living among other young professionals, I could feel the prosperity around me. Gone are those days.

Once, when my business was struggling, to make a school tuition payment I took the large diamond earrings given to me in the late 90s by a boyfriend to a jewelry center that had advertised it would pay cash for diamonds and gold. I had arrived just before the close of the business, and a primped-up saleswoman with bleached blond hair and matching tan leather skirt and shoes looked at the earrings and asked me if she could take them and check on something. I agreed, and when she came back she said she could offer me $80 for the pair. Shocked, I told her "no" and left. Once home, I went to put my earrings back into my jewelry box. I could see they were now tiny and lifeless, no longer large and brilliant. She had switched the earrings. Too embarrassed and exhausted to do anything about what had occurred, I let the situation go, deciding I would buy myself some new earrings when I had the money again. A few months down the line I heard from an elderly neighbor that she'd taken a ring there to sell and she believed they had given her back a ring with a smaller diamond. I never told her about my experience.

And all of this struggle has probably had an impact on my health as well. In an Associated Press poll conducted in 2008, among those who indicated they had "high debt stress" 27 percent had digestive-tract problems and 29 percent said they had experienced severe anxiety. People used to look shocked when I told them I was in my 40s, remarking how I looked at least 10 years younger. I haven't gotten any comments like that in recent years.

Indeed, it's believed people who are stigmatized because of economic, racial and ethnic differences have higher rates of illness, impairment and death than the rest of society on a national and global basis.[21]

While I tick off a couple boxes making me more vulnerable to poverty such as being a woman and single, those who are African-American or Hispanic, have physical challenges or are young, also face additional risks.

And if I, as an educated woman, am being traumatized by the pressure, stigma and stress of poverty, I can only imagine how much more difficult it must be for people who are older and can't negotiate business. Other challenges face single mothers with little schooling, or individuals who have little sense of power for other reasons. In the end, everyone is vulnerable.

And it's hard to ask for help. I personally found it difficult to approach the subject of generational poverty, as it required me to step forward with my own experiences. It required me to look at the mistakes my family and I have made in trying to negotiate our situation.

In fact, my mother refused government help twice.

My mother refused to accept Title 19 shortly after her mastectomy in 2015. She said her job in the billing office at the hospital showed her that people receiving public assistance receive a lower level of care, and a less respectful approach by the hospital staff.

After my mom had a TIA (transient ischemic attack, or mini stroke) in September of 2018, she received visits from a social worker connected to the hospital and seemed willing to talk. A so-called "IRIS" program, which is described on the program website as "a Medicaid Home and Community-Based Services (HCBS) waiver for self-directed long-term supports"[7] would have allocated a budget that would allow for the hiring of care assistance, upgrades to her living situation such as grab bars, and cleaning help.

But when the day arrived for the Milwaukee County "Human Service Worker" from the Department on Aging to meet with us, my mother returned to her usual proud and stubborn stance on the matter, even dumping her head to one side of the chair and refusing to talk with the county representative. It was exactly what I had feared would happen. She'd refused Medicaid and the help it represented once again.

The first time she refused to apply for the program, I started going through the laundry list of things I do each day for my mom, which includes the laundry and everything else, as I am alone in taking care of her. I do her dishes, clean her floors, make her food and set her up in the refrigerator with "emergency sandwiches" and pre-made meals. I pick up her pills, sort her pills, take her to appointments for six different doctors, manage her eye drops, take care of her bills, banking and taxes, take out her garbage, take care of her bird, make sure my mom is clean, do the laundry, make sure the furnace/AC is working correctly (if it's too hot or too cold she'll turn haphazardly on the dials and try to adjust the temps herself).

On the first visit, the county worker told me that since my mom was "still so verbose, there isn't a judge that would say she can't speak for herself."

The second time she refused the help of Title 19, the worker was a somewhat overweight caucasian woman. She wore Harry Potter-like glasses, a navy jacket and a skirt along with heels. Eyes wide under those glasses, she had a somewhat alarmed look as she surveyed the slight state of disarray in my mom's living room. She noted that my mom's chair had become the master-control center. Mom had everything around the chair that she needed - phone, TV remote, kleenex box, eye drops, water glass, soda bottles, hair brush, pressure socks, blankets and pill case. Not being able to move around much on her own meant things had to be positioned so she was able to reach them if alone.

I asked this worker what would happen if I would just tell the county that I couldn't do it all anymore, that I'm no longer able to care for my mother and balance work. Without a moment of consideration, the 30-something woman shot back that the county would then begin a process of filing elder abuse charges against me.

This refusal of help by my mother fueled some animosity on my part. One day when my mom was barking orders at me, complaining that I hadn't gotten her one of the items on her grocery list, I just broke down.

"I'm a person, mom. I'm not a robot!" I yelled. "Remember me, YOUR DAUGHTER? I can't keep doing this!"

Meantime, my mom is making something of a name for herself on the rehab circuit. An intake person at a rehab center recently told a social worker at the hospital that she thought my mom "may be happier somewhere else," considering she didn't seem very satisfied with the facility or staff when she was there.

After my mom had her TIA, and the nurse approached us with a list of potential rehab centers to which she could be transferred, the list of actual possibilities dwindled very quickly. That first choice center was no longer available to us because they had more or less banned my mom.

We also had to eliminate all centers that wouldn't take Medicare, which was probably about 60 percent of the centers within a reasonable distance. Then the social worker had to make calls to see which places actually had beds.

That left me one day scouting three possible places. One I knew of, a large facility west of Milwaukee close to the county zoo that is well known but sometimes receives questionable reviews online. A second was so far to drive I didn't even want to have to make the trip to check it out. A third was in a city in Milwaukee county called St. Francis. St. Francis is close to Lake Michigan, and has a population of just under 10,000. The median household income there is $43,065.

The administrator for the south side place was chipper and warm when she greeted me. The building felt like a long ranch house inside and out and there was a large case with birds in the lobby.

Something I didn't think my mom would like was that she would have a roommate. I decided the place would do in a pinch though, as I was running out of time to find a place to put her. The hospital said they planned to discharge her the next day.

When I arrived at the facility with my mom the following day, however, we were given sideways looks by a group of young women smoking cigarettes and standing at the corner of the potholed parking lot.

When we walked into the building, I spotted the birds and tried to soften my mom up to the place by taking her past their oversized cage.

Then we walked to the administrator's office, but were met by a closed door. Oh, she's gone for the day, said a woman sweeping the floor in the hall. "She is?" I asked. "Because we just arrived and I need to check my mom in."

"Oh, someone else can take care of that," she said. "The program supervisor is just on her break now but will be back." I tried to stay upbeat with my mom as the minutes passed and we waited for the supervisor to come back. Sure enough, the program supervisor who checked us in was one of the women from the parking lot. She reeked of smoke.

Things only went downhill from there. She quickly handed us a packet of papers that she said needed to be signed before my mom could be admitted. One page said my mom agreed to give up her doctor as prescriber of her medications and leave all prescriptions and health evaluations up to the physician connected with the facility. This would also be the physician that would decide when my mom would go home.

I asked the rehab worker if we could sign some, but not all, of the intake papers and was told they all had to be signed or my mom wouldn't be able to stay. I looked outside; it was already dark and I doubted I would be able to hoist my mom up the stairs into her home.

Another sheet said my mom would be liable for payment of at least three days past the date the intake papers were signed, regardless of how long she stayed in the facility.

Begrudgingly, I advised my mom to sign the papers, and she did. A member of the staff then led my mom and me into her room. The room was dark and the TV playing the theme song to the local news was on loud - really loud. A strawberry pink curtain had been drawn and it cut the room to just along my mom's bed, leaving my mom about a fourth of the space in the room. The TV was on the other person's side of the room. Immediately, my mom started talking about how she was feeling claustrophobic. I sat on my mom's bed Indian style, curtain on my back, as long as I could. Eventually, my mom told me to leave because she was worried about me walking around alone in the parking lot when it was so late. Before I left, I took my mom to the group bathroom that was down the hall. A man stumbled in while my mom was only partially clothed.

I ended up discharging my mother from the facility at about 6 p.m. the following day. My mother had called me and said the medical personnel at the facility told her they were going to give her a chest x-ray. She said that when she refused, both the nurse there and the doctor told her they had spoken to me, and I had authorized the x-ray and said she should have it. This was not true.

When I asked to speak to the nurse on the phone and told the nurse I had not spoken with them or authorized an x-ray, the nurse told me that it didn't even matter that I hadn't spoken with them, because the paperwork I'd signed authorized them to perform an x-ray anyway. I do not have power of attorney over my mother, and did not sign any of her paperwork.

Because the staff members had not respected my mother's wishes as she refused a medical treatment/procedure (I could hear a male voice in her room saying "this will just take a minute" as my mother yelled "No!, No!" in the background on the phone while I talked to the female medical representative) and they misrepresented to my mother that I had been involved with a decision to give her an x-ray, I came and removed my mother from the facility.

I later said in an email to the head of the rehab facility that I had deemed it was not a safe environment for my mom, and the staff's refusal to honor her right to refuse a medical procedure/treatment was in violation of Wisconsin law.

When we were packing up at the facility, a nurse explained this all occurred because my mother had said she wouldn't take a tuberculosis (TB) skin test. I said that my mother had been tested thoroughly for the potential for all infections, including TB, before they gave her chemotherapy in conjunction with her mastectomy for breast cancer. You can't have any infection present in your body at the time that you receive chemo, or an infection would spread everywhere once the chemo drugs lower the immune system.

As we were leaving, a female medical representative shouted at us that since we were discharging against medical advice, she would not give us my mother's medications. My mom and I pushed by her with my mom's walker and belongings and I snarled at her "You don't scare me lady." Some of the medications had followed us from the hospital. An aide later quietly handed us one of the eye drop bottles as we left.

After leaving the facility, we went directly to a walk-in health center for a wellness check. The rehab center's representative would not cooperate with the doctor there when the doctor tried to call and find out which medications my mother had already been given for the day, her blood pressure medication and diabetes medications being the biggest concerns.

The doctor at the walk-in center said she had been told that since my mom had been discharged from the rehab facility, the staff was no longer able to talk about her case. We then submitted a formal written request - signed by my mother - through the walk-in center to access her medical records held at the rehab center. It was my mother's legal right to submit such a request and obtain her records. We never did receive a response to that request.

We didn't hear anything more from the rehab facility until five months later, when my mom received a statement from Medicare in the mail. The statement said Medicare would pay the rehab facility $166 for prescriptions.

Doctors also haven't been much of a help. The days surrounding my mother's stroke scare proved that theory.

On the day my mother's TIA occurred, it was an afternoon in late summer of 2018 and we were just about to watch a movie together in her living room. I was talking with my mother about which movie she might like to watch, and suddenly her speech began turning into gibberish.

"I mahh fwahh tun et," she said. She was sitting in her favorite armchair. When the slurred speech happened, I jumped out of my seat so I could look straight on at my mom's face. I couldn't see any evidence of drooping on either side of her face, but she touched her right cheek and said "My fwace feez a liddle fwunny."

My mom snapped out of whatever had happened pretty quickly and scuffled to the bathroom with her walker. "Mom, I think I'm going to have to call 911," I said. "I'm sorry, I know you just got back from the hospital, but I don't know if you are alright or not."

Telling her what I was about to do was a mistake. She launched into a tirade, claiming I was just looking for more reasons to put her back into the hospital.

I did call 911 though and a female 911 operator started firing off little questions and directions I should share with my mom. I led her through these prompts, all while my mother was sitting on the toilet.

Smile.

Do you know what the date is?

Raise both arms.

My mom passed all of these tests and returned to the living room, but the 911 operator continued to dispatch an emergency unit to come out.

Once there, a group of paramedics surrounded my mom in her chair. They asked me what had happened. I told them. I heard one paramedic tell another that my mom had failed nine of the stroke tests. I wasn't sure if that was nine out of 10, but I guessed that wasn't a good thing. I then heard the same gentleman turn to my mom. "Okay, hon, we need to take you to the hospital. You may have had a small stroke."

They then carried my mom down her porch steps in one of the emergency unit's wheelchairs. She was still dressed in her little blue cotton nightgown and grippy socks. I thought about how less than an hour before that we had been sitting cozy in front of the TV. I was about to give her the movie choices of *West Side Story* or *Driving Miss Daisy*.

The ambulance sat outside my mom's place for a long time. I waited until the ambulance left and then locked up and went to the hospital.

At the hospital, I found my mom laying in a bed in one of the emergency room examination areas. She looked very pale. There was an IV in her arm. "Are you the daughter? She was looking for you," a nurse said.

A female physician's assistant (PA) came in and told me they wanted to do a series of tests on my mom, including a CT scan of her head and MRI, in order to confirm if my mom really had a stroke. They also needed to determine if there were blockages.

Mom's blood pressure was 240 over something, which seemed to alarm the nurse in the room. Every so often her stats machine would start emitting a persistent beep.

After about an hour, the PA returned to the room to say she had spoken with my mom's primary care doctor, and he recommended my mom be sent home. The tests could be done through visits to the office.

Stunned, I said I didn't think I would feel comfortable taking my mom home so quickly after what had occurred. In addition, by this point she had become so weak that I didn't think I would be able to get her back up the stairs.

The PA said she would call the doctor back, and in a few minutes she came back into the room, with the doctor on the phone. I held the heavy plastic silver handset, feeling helpless once again as I waited to hear the decision.

"Your mother can take these tests outside of the hospital," he said.

I told him my concerns about taking her home. He listened. He made a remark about how doctors like himself shouldn't have to be put in such a position. Then he hung up the phone - click. The PA left the room. I still didn't know what would happen.

Minutes later, the PA said my mom would be admitted to the hospital. She said the doctor recommended my mom also go to rehab for at least a few days to get stronger again. When we received the intake forms, however, the forms said she had been admitted under an observational status.

I went home and did some reading on what being admitted under an observational status would mean for Medicare coverage at a rehab center. It turned out Medicare beneficiaries must pay almost all of their skilled rehab facility expenses if they are admitted after being classified under an observation status at the hospital.

I called my mom's doctor the next morning and confided in him. I told him how my family would not be able to pay for rehab out of pocket, should my mother leave the hospital directly after an observational status. I asked if he could have her admitted to the hospital and noted Medicare would then cover any rehab. He listened. I felt better after I had spoken with him.

Later that morning when I went into the hospital to see my mom, however, I found her sitting upright in a lounge chair with a new purple band added to the other hospital bands on her left wrist.

The purple band said "DNR" in large bold letters. My mom held her wrist with her other hand, and said "They put this on me. I don't think it's right."

It wasn't right. My mom had filled out forms expressing her wishes should she not be able to speak for herself. She did want to be resuscitated. My heart racing, I ran to the nurses desk. The numb look they gave me told me I wasn't telling them anything they didn't already know.

I aimed my anger at the nurse standing closest to me. "My mother spent the last couple years fighting breast cancer. She had a mastectomy," I yelled with my voice cracking. "She's been fighting to survive!"

I asked for someone to bring a scissors so I could cut the band off of my mom's wrist. Instead, a nurse brought another silver cordless phone handset into the room. My mom's primary care doctor - the same one I had called that morning - was on the line.

"I don't know what you expect me to do for you," he purred into the phone. "You are tired and your family can't keep taking care of her. She has a lot of health problems now."

I explained to him that this was not his decision to make.

At that point, I went into survival mode. I focused solely on the struggle to regain control to keep my mom alive. I felt hot anger that filled up every part of my body and gave me energy.

After we cut the DNR band off of my mom's arm, we asked to have another doctor be in charge of my mom's care in the hospital. The hospitalist on duty took over my mom's medications, but I tried to stick close to my mom in the hospital, arriving early in the morning and leaving as late as I could.

The following Monday, I arrived in my mom's room around 9 a.m. My mom was sitting up in a chair covered with a number of thin blankets. When I sat down next to her, she told me that her original primary care doctor had come into her room earlier in the morning. "He came in and he was yelling at me," she said. "Why doesn't he like me anymore?" She said he had given her a similar speech about how she should wear the bracelet, and she had become a burden to her family.

To make matters worse and even more heartbreaking, my mother was slurring her speech when she told me this. I found out later from the nurse that they had given my mother an anti-anxiety drug to keep her still while they administered a CT scan. No one ever consulted me on the administration of this medication.

There was concern that she had some blockage in her Carotid Artery on her right side. (In the end, we did find out that she has about a 70 percent blockage.)

My mom looked pale and frail, with her hair a swirl of grey and white mats after being slid around on beds and exam tables. All I could think was how she had been attacked by this fiend of a doctor while at her lowest point.

We spent the rest of that day talking to the floor manager at the hospital and filing complaints against the doctor. Even then my mother would stop occasionally and ask the hospital representatives why her doctor didn't like her anymore.

Other than medical stability, locking in some sort of financial stability in terms of my mom's health care has been something that I've been wrestling with for a long time.

What I have done is I made sure I keep up a life insurance policy on myself on which I've named my parents as beneficiaries. I enrolled in this policy a long time ago, thinking that if anything ever happened to me, at least my parents could use the money for care in their elder years. Even that was a compromise, as I'd originally set out to secure long-term health insurance policies for my parents which could pay for services such as nursing home care. The long-term insurance, however, turned out to be something that was simply too cost prohibitive to do.[8]

When days have gotten dark, I've reminded myself that I am not alone. There are others out there trying to care for elderly parents, being pulled back into poverty because of an unfair system and perhaps paying the price with their own physical and mental health. In terms of the group with the largest number of completed suicides, the largest growth area as of 2013 was women age 50 and older.

I wondered how others might be faring as they try to negotiate the system. It's clear people can be taken advantage of because of factors such as age, race or education leve

I never knew.

That is, I never could see the whole Milwaukee story - about its systemic problems - until now, or at least I'm starting to learn it. The truth is that Milwaukee is deeply divided by economic status and race. It's a city that tends to focus on part of its population, but not all of it. The results of that blindsightedness show in comparisons to other parts of the country.

Milwaukee is a hypersegregated area. What this means is that a single race - in this case African-Americans - are isolated and concentrated in certain areas. The isolated group also tend to live in urban areas.[22] [23] The group tends to be cut off from opportunities and resources that lend social and economic support.[24]

Wisconsin ranks 47th out of U.S. states for per capita public health funding.[34] According to a 2015 Robert Wood Johnson Foundation report, each year just over 3,000 deaths in Wisconsin could be avoided if the state's inhabitants had more equal access to health care.

Statistically speaking, Wisconsin is ranked as the worst in the country when it comes to excessive drinking, with almost a quarter of its residents said to drink to excess. There are constant cases of wrong-way drunk drivers on the expressway (370 from 2012 to 2017), which lead to deaths and severe injuries. (I won't even drive on the expressway in Wisconsin.) Wisconsin also leads the nation in terms of Whooping Cough cases, and this is despite the fact there is a vaccine to prevent the illness. Wisconsin ranks number 21 in terms of rates of obesity in the nation.

In 2017, a smaller number of children in the state of Wisconsin had health insurance than they did the previous year.

Wisconsin has not completely expanded Medicaid. There is an obvious relationship between the poor health outcomes in Wisconsin and the state's failure to provide insurance for those who fall into a lower income bracket.

In a tendril of crossing bars, the poverty rates for U.S. children across the states play out in the U.S. Census Bureau's poverty rates or income trend map, with data last recorded in 2016. (The gap between 2004 and 2005 is due to a change in data collection efforts.) It certainly appears a child has more of a chance of living in poverty should he or she live in one state compared to another state, with some of the highest poverty rates reported in The South.[12]

The graph shows that in 2016 19.5 percent of those under 18 in the U.S live in poverty. The state of Wisconsin was below the national average on the U.S. census map at a 15.7 percent poverty rate among children in the age group. While some would see the fact Wisconsin ranks better than the national average for this rate as somewhat encouraging, stunning is the fact that in the major metropolitan area of Milwaukee, one of the least poverty-ridden areas for this age group sits right next to an area with some of the most poverty.

As of 2014, African-American babies were about three times more likely than caucasian infants to die in Milwaukee.[38] As of 2018, the state of Wisconsin showed the same average, with Wisconsin's Infant Mortality Rate for

African-Americans ranked as the highest in the U.S. The chronic stress and

conditions of poverty are reasons commonly given for the high rate in the state.[39]

According to data from the U.S. National Center for Health Statistics and

the Robert Wood Johnson Foundation, health is influenced by conditions even block

to block.[56] Divisions are clear in Milwaukee, where the neighborhoods are highly

segregated by race and economic factors.

To see this for myself, I punched the address for the River Hills Village

Hall - 7650 N Pheasant Ln, Milwaukee, WI 53217 - into Google Maps on my phone.

I omitted the option of taking the freeway from the mapping, and was given

directions to my destination.

The mapping system led me through an older part of the city, on North

Hawley Road, then down West Lloyd Street, and finally down North Sherman

Boulevard for a little over six miles.

After turning right onto Good Hope Road and driving a little over two

miles, I was at my destination in River Hills. In the 53217 zip code, located 15

minutes from the center of Milwaukee, the median price of homes is about $700,000.

Described by one traveler's guide as "bucolic," the crime rate in the area is 71

percent lower than the national average.

About 10 miles away, in zip code 53206, it's estimated children born in

the area will live on average 12 years less than children born in zip code 53217. The area has become infamous for having one of the highest incarceration rates of African-American men.

Driving down Sherman Boulevard I could see dilapidated buildings and I felt the long history of economic struggle.

This was the second time in a rather short timeframe I had visited the block of streets on the North Side. Only the previous October I had been in the area delivering photocopies of my mom's social security statements at the Energy Assistance office there. My mom had applied for heating assistance for the winter season, but when that assistance never showed up on her heating bill, we were told her forms had never arrived in the mail. The forms would have to be delivered that day in order to meet the deadline to receive help.

While there are some very large historic houses in the Sherman Park area, on this most recent visit to the area I pulled to the side of the road to take a picture of a rather utilitarian-looking public housing unit. I drove away quickly, struck by how my desire to document difficult conditions and leave was disgusting.

When I was a child, I heard my parents talking about the "Inner Core" or Milwaukee's North side.[13] I didn't know the history though, or why African-Americans seemed concentrated in a certain area.

I did witness the hatred, however. My father, of Western European descent, would talk with great anger about the "Blacks" that would throw rocks at my grandmother when she would sweep her front steps at her home on 20th and Walnut. I had no concept of why there was tension between the groups, however.[14]

My dad used to say that when he and his brothers were growing up in the area, there were no "Blacks." History accounts about Milwaukee show that between the early '30s when my dad was born, and the early '70s, when I was born, Milwaukee's African-American population increased by around 700 percent[15] as many African-Americans left The South and entered the city looking for jobs at the many tanneries, manufacturers and breweries.

According to University of Wisconsin-Milwaukee records, from 1920 to 1945 alone, the African-American population of the city jumped from around 2,000 to around 10,200. Attempts to bring in African-American workers to break strikes (done with the Illinois Steel strike of 1919 and Milwaukee Road Strike of 1920) came to an end when Dan Hoan, a Socialist mayor, got involved and stopped the practice.[16] Similar practices were seen in Chicago and Northwest Indiana.

Much like in other rust belt cities that were once focused on industry and steel production, a need for workers during both world wars opened up jobs for people of color and women. When the job market started to tighten, competition for work fueled some of the suspicions and animosities among Milwaukee's racial and social classes.

My father's family owned a large house on the North side of Milwaukee where my father grew up.

While no members of my family live in the area at this point (the house was sold after my grandmother's death "for a song," according to my dad), I frequently hear about the area on Milwaukee's nightly news - and sometimes the national news. Years of economic decline have led to sharp divides and deadly streets. On the news I see constant reports of double shootings, co-sleeping deaths (in 2017 Milwaukee's medical examiner said "half of the infant deaths in Milwaukee County were because of unsafe sleep" situations)[17], hit-and-runs and fires. In 2016, a shooting of an African-American man by a Milwaukee police officer led to three days of protests and fires in the Sherman Park area on Milwaukee's north side.[18] For many, the incident brought to mind the civil rights riot from the '60s (dubbed the "Long Hot Summer of 1967" when African-Americans protested police brutality and housing discrimination.)[19]

Shootings of African-American men by police continue to grow in the Milwaukee area, as they have in many other cities. Police in the U.S. killed 164 African-American people in the first eight months of 2020 alone.

While the number of hypersegregated metro areas in the U.S. dropped by about 50 percent since the 1970s,[25] this has not been the case in Milwaukee.

Statistics[26] indicate that about 70 percent of Milwaukee Public School students are "children of color." Milwaukee's former superintendent of public schools, Darienne Driver, left her job in 2018 to take a position as president and CEO of the United Way in Southeastern Michigan, but not before she participated in a forum on addressing health disparities at Marquette University and gave some impassioned comments. She noted at one point that it's important to educate the whole child and be aware of the intersections of poverty and violence and health.

Detroit was where Driver, a short African-American woman with a captivating smile and go-get em attitude, started her career as a teacher around 20 years ago. She became interim school superintendent in Milwaukee in July 2014 and was named permanently to the position later that same year when she was 36.

When I caught up with Driver months after she left Milwaukee (her assistant said Driver's schedule was "packed," and I believe it. Driver ate her lunch when we were able to connect on a call), I asked Driver if since she started working with the educational system she noticed improvements in public health of children. "We still have a long way to go," she said. She added that when she first left Milwaukee she had to switch gears and take some time to get her head out of the problems of the city.

And in regard to the hypersegregation, Driver said in the years since she became involved in Milwaukee, the situation "hasn't gotten better." And she added, "It kills me to say that. Unfortunately, we still haven't figured out how to build that bridge and establish some kind of sustainable trust over time."

And "in Milwaukee, you have a city that was designed to be segregated… Those ghosts are still haunting us," she said.

I wondered what she meant by saying the city was set up to be segregated. I looked into the history of Milwaukee and segregation. I assumed the stance of someone looking at the poverty issues of Milwaukee in a new way as a returned journalist and as someone dealing with my mother's struggles as well as my own.

In Milwaukee, systemic racism was supported by the housing situation, as it not only segregated whites and African-Americans, but also kept African-Americans from being able to purchase homes outside of some neighborhoods, where there were codes and redlining by banks. The situation made it almost impossible for African-American workers in the city to gain wealth through obtaining real estate, as they were unable to purchase homes in affluent areas and see their investments grow.

A report by the Metropolitan Integration Research Center indicated that "at least 16 of the 18 Milwaukee County suburbs were using *racially restrictive covenants* to exclude" home ownership by African-Americans by the 1940s. When a family would buy a home and accompanying plot of land in a suburb, they would be asked to sign a covenant promising they would not "sell, lease or otherwise convey their property to certain groups for a specified time period, often 20-25 years."[27]

Such covenants were filed with the county register of deeds and became a court matter when breached.[28]

And even data that are gathered in an attempt to shine a light on challenges to create change can be used to lock in trends of segregation of housing. One of the first places I saw the Child Opportunity Index report mentioned was through a story link contained in a social media posting by a North Shore Chicago real estate agent. He was trying to talk up the North Shore as a haven from the troubles of other areas.

The Robert Wood Johnson Foundation's Mallya said there are also experiences that African-American people have throughout their lifetime in this country that are different compared to what other races experience. A telephone survey done in 2017 for the Robert Wood Johnson Foundation, National Public Radio and the Harvard T.H. Chan School of Public Health found that half or more of 802 African-Americans who participated in the survey said they have been discriminated against when interacting with police, at work in regard to getting paid or getting a promotion, and in the way cases have been processed in the U.S. legal system.

"Race matters in our country because of all the ways that people treat you - your access to resources, how the courts treat you - the entire system treats you differently," Mallya said.

And the way this system treats you differently could certainly impact your health care.

In a Wisconsin Department of Health Services publication titled "Healthiest Wisconsin 2020 Baseline and Health Disparities,"[57] a more than 1,000-page report aimed at identifying health disparities in the state, it was said that "historical trauma," or "the cumulative exposure to traumatic events that not only affect the individual exposed, but continue to affect subsequent generations" is believed to impact not only African-Americans, but also "American Indians, Hispanics/Latinos, Asians, immigrants and refugees, war veterans, and families experiencing generational poverty."

According to the report, this trauma plays out as mistrust of legal, health care, and educational systems. The report makes it clear that poverty is a public health issue as it affects people's bodies.

If you have these mistrusts, it can lead to "worse overall health and mental health outcomes, less of a sense of safety at school, neighborhood, and personal levels, and higher rates of risk behaviors including alcohol and drug abuse, suicide, homicide, and domestic violence, according to the report.

This can also lead to higher rates of chronic diseases with worse outcomes, "including for stroke, diabetes, high cholesterol, and asthma," according to the report.

In addition, the report found that "children with access to places for safe physical activity during non-school hours are more likely to be physically active."

According to the National Center for Children in Poverty, about one in three African-American, Hispanic, and Native-American children lives under the poverty line in the U.S. This compares to about one in 10 caucasian children. In Wisconsin, almost half of all African-American children live in poor families.[33]

In Wisconsin, Hispanic and African-American families are most at risk for not having health insurance.[35]

And while some initiatives in the area have found legs, others have not. Milwaukee's Black Health Coalition of Wisconsin, an entity that is comprised of 26 health care and social service organizations and African-American individual members, in 2014 lost $750,000 to fund its Eliminating Racial and Ethnic Disparities program. The program had been focused on narrowing the disparities in Milwaukee's infant mortality rate.

The Child Opportunity Index (COI) attempts to measure health opportunity for children in terms of socioeconomic, environmental and educational opportunity. According to Diversitydatakids, the organization that publishes the data, this data set clearly shows that opportunity is closely aligned to income in the Wisconsin area.

But how exactly the current political climate might impact health programs and outcomes remains to be seen.

The Kaiser report said that "many challenges remain to address social determinants of health, and new directions pursued by the Trump Administration could limit resources and initiatives focused on these efforts."

The Trump Administration introduced plans to expand work requirements associated with public programs[40] and reduce funding for prevention and public health,[41] the report noted. Media reports have indicated children are not clear of being targeted.

>**Chapter 4: The Body Bears A History**

Ill health at the time a baby is born and into childhood is one way poverty is passed from one generation to another. Insufficient health care can be evidenced on an individual's body throughout life. But in the broader picture, physical effects are only superficial. The injuries that can really debilitate are the physiological and emotional blows.

Even a little insurance and a little care are better than none. It was a great relief when my mother qualified for Medicare after going most of her life without any health insurance at all because the insurance was financially out of reach.

I recorded the following account from my mother a few years ago as a part of another project, but with my new perspective on generational poverty, it seems telling about how untreated conditions in childhood due to inadequate health care affects children into adulthood.

"I was eight years old. I was told by a neighbor that I could practice riding on their bike - a woman's bike with foot brakes - while they went inside to eat supper. I was delighted.

It was a big red bike, and my legs barely touched the pedals. I was doing fine, and I rode back and forth on the sidewalk. My legs started to get tired, so I thought I would slow down and sit, but my legs were not long enough. I tried to push down to stop, and when I did, the back wheel came up and pitched me over the handlebars and into the air. I flew and landed on the cement. I hurt my chin, arms and legs. They were all scratched up. I was worried about the bike though, and was relieved when it seemed untouched. Then I picked it up and took it back.

I went home. My sister, Evelyn, was the only one there. I climbed onto the couch. My mother came home later. Nobody ever really looked me over. There were a lot of kids to take care of, and it was around the time of The Depression. But later I realized that when I'd fallen on the cement, I had hurt my spine. Later in life a chiropractor called it a "curvature of the spine." There was a possible surgery, but it was so dangerous I decided not to do it. I also needed the money to take care of you kids."

I've seen pictures, and the truth is that when my mom was in her 20s she looked

like quite the delicate pinup girl. A leggy Snow White with a lovely warm look in her

eyes. Slowly but surely, the back abnormality and time have taken a toll. These days she's considerably bent to the side, and walking is done only when absolutely necessary and with a walker. I often wish the people who care for my mother at medical facilities could see the photo, and acknowledge all that she has been in her life. I wish they could give her the respect she deserves.

My mom currently lives in a home just about big enough for her and her little bird. Even that is too much, however, when it comes to the usual upkeep of a yard and property.

The place is in somewhat of a shambles. Mom sometimes confuses old food with new food, so I try to make sure the old food disappears. I sometimes find empty soup cans in the vegetable drawer in the fridge. I don't even want to know why.

Real life for us includes that my mother can't keep her bills straight anymore. I've spent countless hours trying to figure out her energy bill, cell phone bill and health insurance. I started taking her to have her taxes done yearly at a special AARP volunteer tax prep session for seniors at the library.

It's a constant job of plate spinning to keep things from being turned off or canceled. At first I was giving my name and identifying myself as my mother's daughter when I would call billing representatives. Later I realized that should my mother ever not be available, they would likely come looking for me.

My mother is not alone in trying to live alone. According to the Administration on Aging, as of 2014, about 30 percent of noninstitutionalized persons over 65 lived by themselves. That was 8.8 million women and 3.8 million men. Further, as of 2014, almost half of older women 75 and over lived alone.

Also worth noting is that treating illnesses to prolong life has become a double-edged sword, of sorts. The 85+ population is projected to more than double from six million in 2013 to 14.6 million in 2040. Where will all of these people live? Who will take care of them?

And government statistics released in 2018 show birth rates declining in every age group except those women in their 40s. As women wait until later to have children, children of older parents are likely to one day find themselves actively taking care of a declining parent while still at a busy stage of life themselves. Gone are the days of the 60-something retiree driving to see mom or dad in the nursing home. Here are the days of dealing with the problems of aging parents while you are still smack dab in the thick of it in your own life.

>**Chapter 5: The Fate Of The City Where I Grew Up**

Why do inequities continue to persist in Milwaukee and Wisconsin? It appears it is largely because of policies that support a small number of people holding most of the cards. While a few are winning, a large number are left with losing hands.

I've realized that felt experience alters how we understand human problems. Empathy fosters more action than sympathy.

I believe in order to make changes in Milwaukee, the "othering" of some facets of the community by those in power needs to stop. The only way this will ever happen is if power players realize it could be them or their families who are experiencing the same hardships, just as I realized this could happen to me.

How important is this? At the current time, a child would likely have a different expected lifespan depending upon where he or she lives.[58]

According to information collected by the American Academy of Pediatrics, "neighborhood child opportunity was negatively associated with visits for respiratory conditions, asthma, assault, and ambulatory care-sensitive conditions but positively associated with injury-related visits."[59]

As I am learning, inadequate health care in different periods of a person's life can have a lasting impact. When individuals don't get "nonessential" tests for things like allergies, their hearing and mental health, it can greatly impact them in later life and their income potential.

I wanted to see for myself some of the services that are being offered to low-income Milwaukee residents.

City on a Hill

City on a Hill is a non-profit organization based in the Milwaukee area on a former hospital campus. Religious principles are stressed, and the organization attempts to provide help with free health clinics that include foot care, a vision clinic and physical therapy, housing and youth programs.

I was told an average of 200 individuals attend these health clinics at the center. They are attended to by more than 100 volunteers that serve the health clinic, which I was told had 2,578 visits in 2018.

To get a feel for how the organization works, I volunteered at the free health clinic one Saturday in February. I stood behind a long row of tables with a handful of other volunteers. It was our job to get people checked into the clinic. That is, we made sure the members of the community were aware of which services were available and marked slips to say they wanted the services. Attendees of the clinic then took the slips with them when they walked to the tables where services were performed. We also pulled the file for each member of the community who came in to get services and we updated their information. Some had listed the name and phone number of a local shelter as their home. I helped check in maybe 20 people in the course of the day. Each would line up at the door when they arrived and then approach the row of white plastic tables when it was their turn.

At City on a Hill, I stood next to a sunny window, still layered in all of the clothing that I'd put on to fend off the elements of the 7-degree F or so Wisconsin winter day.

The individuals who came in wore many layers as well and also remarked about how hot it was in that corner. Many of their coats, however, were marked up (possibly with tar from being against cement, I guessed).

The community members that I took in had all been there before, and I was told most of the people who attend do tend to be "regulars" as the center aims to serve the community surrounding the facility, and most of the publicity about the center is word of mouth. While about 80 percent of the attendees were African-American, the rest seemed about equally divided between whites and Hispanics.

Each attendee was given a little blue sheet and I would go through the checklist with each of them. The choices were: Blood Pressure, Blood Sugar, Doctor Visit, Height/Weight/BMI, Clinical Breast Exam, Health Education: Healthy Heart (a gift of a Kleenex box was given if they chose this one - something which seemed to make most jump at the chance to sign up), Smoking Cessation Information/Assistance, Dental Hygiene Information, Physical Therapy, Social Work (assistance with community referrals), Medical College of Wisconsin's Health

Outreach Programs, Health Care Navigation Assistance (help with signing up for BadgerCare), Hygiene Pantry (which everyone signed up for) Food Pantry (another choice no one turned down), Meal (also popular) and Prayer. On that last item, after signing up for the prayer one individual looked at me and asked if I had prayed that day. I had, as the director lead all of us in a prayer before we came out to help.

"Help us all to remember that each person deserves dignity and respect, and that they are coming to us at a particular time of vulnerability in their lives. Bless these volunteers for putting themselves in a vulnerable position in dealing with these people who need our help."

The center is very close to Marquette University and many of the volunteers there were either medical or dental students or instructors from Marquette or other universities in the general vicinity, including Carthage College.

"This is a great opportunity for students to get some experience," City on a Hill Operations Director Brooke Chapman told me. "It's also good for the kids to come into contact with kids who are in college, particularly African-American students who had made a transition out of poverty."

I graduated in the mid '90s from Marquette with a Bachelor's degree in Journalism and minor in English. I paid for school partially by working when I wasn't in class, and partially with an academic scholarship. I later repeated the work and school split when I earned my Master's degree in Creative Writing from

Northwestern. One of my biggest takeaways from Northwestern? A comment from Professor Ivy Wilson who teaches courses on the comparative literatures of the black diaspora and U.S. literary studies: "Education is one of the few things they can never take away from you."

The City on a Hill director explained to me later that there is a large fear of diabetes by most of the attendees of the center because many of them have seen a friend or relative lose a limb to the disease. Also, according to the American Heart Association, over 40 percent of African-American men and women have problems with high blood pressure.

I was given a ticket for lunch, and when I was there I took the opportunity to sit with one of the members of the community I'd met. He was caucasian. He was missing many teeth. His hair looked unkempt and greasy. Yet he seemed quite interested in chatting up any of the female volunteers.

I asked him about finding services, if he knew where to go. He told me that when it was cold the previous week (with temperatures as cold as -23F with the latest Polar Vortex) he went to the library to get warm. It was when he was there he used the computers to find out where he could stay for the night. Actually, he struck me as being pretty savvy. I wondered how most would find the shelter they need, if they have to look on a computer to find the locations and times.

While the libraries in the Milwaukee area don't keep records regarding how many people use their facilities, they do serve as shelter from the elements during the day and can provide information on other services available.

In December of 2018, it was announced that "warming rooms" in Milwaukee would receive $75,000 to operate from the city's Housing Trust Fund. The funding followed a protest by the "Street Angels Milwaukee " volunteer group that aims to aid Milwaukee's homeless community members - of which there were an estimated 5,027 as of January of 2017.

Later in the day when I was in the director's office talking with her, Chapman came in and said, "Miss Mabel says she wants to go to detox."

They hemmed and hawed about the right place to take her and discussed how she had checked herself out of other places they had taken her in the past. The director remarked that also because she has "those mental problems" she is a "hard sell" to get in for treatment.

There were bright moments though. A tiny African-American woman with no teeth shuffled slowly down the center of the hallway with a walker, and it was obvious she was a favorite. She appeared to be near her 70s, and couldn't have weighed more than 100 pounds.

"Well, Miss Belle, look at you!" Chapman remarked.
When Chapman turned back to me she had tears in her eyes. "We hadn't seen her in so long, Chapman said. "She's looking good. Put on some weight. Has a nice jacket. Someone at the new facility is taking care of her."

Chapman would tell everyone we passed that she had seen Miss Belle and how good Miss Belle looked. How she had a warm jacket.

An 18-or-so-year-old African-American volunteer named Dantel passed us in the hallway and informed Chapman he was heading out for the day. Once in the rec room, where a pool table sat in the middle of the room and three old large computers lined the wall, Chapman told me she thought that volunteer would be one who would break his family out of the generational poverty cycle.

When he first arrived at the center about 10 years back, he was so withdrawn that he couldn't even look eye-to-eye with the staff members and other members of the community, Chapman explained. His father was in jail. He was trying to stay clear of the gangs that prey upon kids in the area who are looking for a father figure. Many times these kids either end up in the gangs or are used as pawns by the gang members.

Now Dantel excels in public speaking at school and gives presentations to the groups at City on a Hill, Chapman said. She said he's also brought other kids from school to the center and showed them that it is a safe place to come after classes end for the day.

And on the subject of jail, Chapman noted that when individuals are put in jail it significantly impacts the family unit.

"Almost everyone we see has a family member in jail or knows someone who is in jail," she said. And she said that often "people of color don't have a family lawyer" because they are struggling in poverty and they have a hard time getting sufficient representation in legal situations. She said sometimes this results in harsher sentencing. She added that City on a Hill tries to act as an advocate for families

facing legal situations, but doesn't have an official legal program set up.

I asked her which issue she thought needed to be addressed first in order

to break down the impacts of generational poverty. She seemed hard-pressed to come

up with an answer.

"At least in Milwaukee, there are so many issues it's overwhelming," she

said. "You have to figure out which to address first. It's almost like a puzzle."

She said generational poverty is "definitely more present" in the North

side of Milwaukee, "It has significant struggles." She noted that the South Side,

which is primarily Hispanic in terms of the background of its community members,

is also hard hit by economic challenges.

Previous Wisconsin governor Scott Walker refused to set up a

government health exchange in 2012.[63] Walker said that once federal funding

earmarked for the exchange dried up, costs for Wisconsin taxpayers could skyrocket.

Walker also turned away federal funds that would have expanded Medicaid in

2014,[64] again contending accepting the funds could have put the state on the hook for

higher costs down the line.

This all resulted in higher health insurance premium payments for Wisconsin

residents compared to those in nearby states, including Minnesota.

During his campaign for governor, current Wisconsin governor Tony

Evers said he would act to bring down health insurance costs and prescription drug

prices.

He also said he would accept federal Medicaid expansion funds to help insure thousands more in Wisconsin. He would also put funds into preventative health programs and extend protections for pre-existing conditions, including cancer, diabetes and depression.[65]

But as others researching the topic have found, economic and social principles of action also involve what is health policy.

It is the coming together of different facets of society that could help to share concepts that have the potential for aiding children and improving the health outcomes of generations.

Driver had said during our conversation that putting together health care advisory committees is one thing that Milwaukee does well.

Milwaukee governor Evers assembled a group of advisors to help decide how Medicaid expansion money could be put to best use in Wisconsin. Evers' Medicare advisory committee included[66] the office director for Disability Rights Wisconsin in Milwaukee, Barbara Beckert; Kofi Short, community manager of a program called Diverse & Resilient, which focuses on the health needs of bisexual, gay, lesbian, and transgender individuals, and the public policy coordinator for Mental Health America of Wisconsin, Mary Neubauer.

Evers' group also included president of the Foundation for Black Women's Wellness, Lisa Peyton-Caire; Executive Director of the Rural Wisconsin Health Cooperative, Tim Size; and Dr. Dipesh Navsaria, a pediatrician with UW Health.

Medicaid money is important for the health of children, because in

Wisconsin one in three children is covered by Medicaid[67] and just short of half of all

children with disabilities are covered by Medicaid in Wisconsin. An additional

176,000 people would be covered by Medicaid in Wisconsin, should the state accept

expansion.[68] Evers, whose grouping of individuals in his Medicaid health group

appears to come with an acknowledgement of the diversity that is required to address

the current situation, has said he also wishes to expand dental treatment for

low-income residents.

Standards for care with equal opportunity and without discrimination are

mapped out in the Constitution of the the Universal Declaration of Human Rights

from the United Nations and WHO.

Article 25 of the UN's Constitution of the Universal Declaration of

Human Rights says: "Everyone has the right to a standard of living adequate for the

health and well-being of himself and of his family, including food, clothing, housing

and medical care and necessary social services, and the right to security in the event

of unemployment, sickness, disability, widowhood, old age or other lack of

livelihood in circumstances beyond his control."[69]

This article was enacted by the UN in the 1940s, yet here in 2019 the

standards are difficult to nearly impossible for the majority of the world's people to

attain, although the goals should be easy to reach in the U.S. which in 2018 had $98

trillion of the world's $317 trillion in wealth.

Perhaps even more difficult to understand is that in Wisconsin - a state in the one of the top 15 richest countries in the world according to gross domestic product per capita - generational poverty continues to be a problem and health care is substandard and out of reach for thousands.

Amid the broader picture of insurance, over half of children have the coverage of private insurance through their parents plans from work, or through individual plans, according to research from the Kaiser Family Foundation.

>**Chapter 6: Conversations**

Many of the individuals who talked with me started their comments on the difficult issues of child health, racism, and poverty, with a deep breath. This indicated to me each believed there was a great deal to be said, but also wanted to make sure they chose their words carefully. I also felt a sense of exhaustion after dealing with the helplessness and stress of caring for my mom, lack of services, fears connected with the web of debt and the politics involved with organizations that are supposed to be there to assist. There was also the disappointment that other community members don't care, yet claim to believe in justice, moral codes and the Christian principles of love and mercy for everyone - particularly those who have the least among us.

And with so many social services agencies assigned to handle different aspects of urban communities, it's difficult for members of the community to even figure out where they need to go for help.

It's true, when you look up social services agencies on Google you get an incredibly deep pool of options. Try to figure out which of these serve your community and it could take some time. Try to access them without a computer, car or even a telephone and things can get even more difficult.

Many churches come to City on a Hill throughout the year to volunteer and offer significant funding. Volunteers hail from different denominations or are not affiliated with a denomination. In 2018, the organization had 1,362 volunteers from 87 different churches or organizations.

The parent organization of City on a Hill is the Wisconsin Northern Michigan District of the Assemblies of God, and some of City on a Hill's board members are also a part of the parent organization. The Wisconsin Northern Michigan District of the Assemblies of God gifted the property and created City on a Hill in 2000.

Hope House is another organization that I visited in the course of my research, trying to get a handle on what services are accessible in the Milwaukee area for those in need.

When working my way through school at Marquette, a senior crimes reporter at the Journal Sentinel had described the area where Hope House is located as one that is gang-infested, and said I should never be there alone at night. At present day, the area still has a larger number of reported violent crimes at night than other areas, but has become a place of interest for some young professionals moving into the city because of its cheaper housing and a developing restaurant scene.

Hope House provides housing, health care, food, financial assistance and education for both children and adults.

"We have a number of families staying with us right now," said a house manager who identified herself as Norma. Norma sat behind an old wooden desk near a large window. Her desk was covered with piles of pages and clipboards that included a laundry sign-up sheet and sign-in sheet for individuals staying at the shelter.

I asked her if I could go to the free clinic that was being held upstairs and she waved me on. When I opened the door of that office, I was surprised to see there was only one family in the waiting room, a man and woman with a little girl. The child was coughing and was being comforted by her mother who held her wrapped in a blanket. I introduced myself to the woman at the intake desk in the clinic, and she said I would need to talk with the director, who was out on that day.

I went back downstairs. I asked Norma why there weren't more people in the free clinic upstairs. She told me that the doctor who is often there was on leave. But she said even the usual hours don't work for a lot of people.

"All these places close up so early," she said. "Parents can't afford to be leaving work early."

But she said there was also something else. Individuals have to make sure they have the right paperwork in order to see a doctor.

"It's just messed up," she said. "You really have to get your information together to know where to go."

A long wooden bench lined the wall across from Norma's desk, and there were boxes full of loaves of bread. I figured the boxes must have been donated by a local bakery. Soon a pale white woman with a puffy face walked in and started rifling around in the boxes.

"You can't take anything out of there," Norma told her, and the woman kept walking further into the building.

I realized that while some of the individuals who work and volunteer at these organizations are well-off, some also span the other end of the spectrum. There were some indications that a few had challenges in their own lives.

While I was standing in the lobby, Norma received a call on her cell phone. Someone on the other end of the line was trying to convince her to lend them some money.

"Alright, I'll lend it to you when I get paid, but you've got to get it back to me when you get paid," she said to the muffled voice on the line.

I thanked Norma for her time and headed out. She was a very frail, yet graceful African-American woman, likely in her late 50s or 60s. I think I felt every bone in her fingers when I shook her hand.

The director of City on a Hill told me that while the nonprofits involved in helping those who are poverty stricken climb out of their circumstances, no two organizations look exactly alike as they have to be tailored to fit each community and their special challenges.

Successful nationwide projects have included:

The **Harlem Children's Zone**[82] is a project that began in the 1990s and now involves around 20,000 youth and adults, involving community building, education of parents and children, and community support services.

Opportunity Zones are community development projects that connect capital with low-income communities.[8384]

Purpose Built Communities is a project led by a non-profit consulting firm that aims to rebuild neighborhoods experiencing poverty by a number of initiatives by a variety of unrelated players, including mayors, asset managers and those who make policies.

But why have Milwaukee and Wisconsin failed to create an adequate care system for citizens? Why does the government refuse to deal with disparities and do more for its most vulnerable inhabitants?

In terms of the outlook for the city of Milwaukee, there is some hope that the implementation of new policies could make for improvements. With a new administration in Milwaukee there is renewed discussion regarding Milwaukee and Wisconsin's health care and support for public services for areas degraded by economic decline and environmental stresses.

Two months before the election in 2018, Evers gave a State of Education speech as Superintendent of Public Instruction and noted that "education remains - as it has always been - the great equalizer. The pathway to prosperity. The key to a skilled workforce and a robust economy."[4647]

Lieutenant Governor Mandela Barnes' platform included that it's time the city use all federal funding for health care that is available to it. This would mean utilizing the "Obamacare" Medicaid expansion and creating a BadgerCare low income public health care option for all individuals in the state. Right now, individuals must be living under the federal poverty level to qualify.

BadgerCare does not come without controversy, however. There are many stories of people who are on BadgerCare being put on long waiting lists before they can have surgery or see specialists.

Barnes has also said he will push for the minimum wage to be raised in the state. Minimum wage in Wisconsin as of 2019 was $7.25 an hour, in line with the national average.

The reality is the history of aiding the sick and vulnerable goes back, way back. And it wasn't always centered around those designated as healers. The relationship between care of the sick and mercy is seen in early Greek teachings as Greeks saw an importance in caring for the sick, including their sick slaves. Religious moral doctrines are well grounded in the responsibility to care for others. The Torah discussed how God visited Abraham through angels when he was sick. Bikur Cholim is a precept that involves aiding and the sick. In the Muslim religion, humanitarianism is seen as a fundamental principle. It's viewed as an obligation to give aid to someone in distress.[75] As in many religions, Muslims believe there must be a balance in body and spirit to have good health.

Christian religions, which take many of their moral codes from Jewish, Greek and Babylonian roots, believe Jesus Christ himself acted as an example of how to treat those who are in need or sick. The Bible John 9:6-7 "6 After saying this, he spit on the ground, made some mud with the saliva, and put it on the man's eyes.

7 "Go," he told him, "wash in the Pool of Siloam." So the man went and washed, and came home seeing."

There's another example of care by Jesus in The Bible Luke 17:12-16 "12 As he was going into a village, ten men who had leprosy met him. They stood at a distance 13 and called out in a loud voice, "Jesus, Master, have pity on us!" 14 When he saw them, he said, "Go, show yourselves to the priests." And as they went, they were cleansed. 15 One of them, when he saw he was healed, came back, praising God in a loud voice. 16 He threw himself at Jesus' feet and thanked him—and he was a Samaritan."

In religion, mercy became a concept closely tied with care. It does not require a medical degree to bestow mercy. Mercy can come from anyone.

And, in fact, while the Hippocratic oath does not include a promise the medical professionals will "do no harm," as many believe, the modern version of the oath does ask the pledging physician to affirm that they will remember they are a member of society with obligations to their fellow human beings.[76]

After all, how can we, as a people, say we are morally upright humans and yet ignore these tenets that have served as guideposts throughout history?

Endnotes: Newspaper Clippings And Historical Documents

1. *Annual Update of the HHS Poverty Guidelines.* (2018). *Federal Register.*

Retrieved 2 December 2018, from

https://www.federalregister.gov/documents/2018/01/18/2018-00814/annual-update-o

f-the-hhs-poverty-guidelines

2. *Annual Update of the HHS Poverty Guidelines.* (2016). *Federal Register.*

Retrieved 2 December 2018, from

https://www.federalregister.gov/documents/2016/01/25/2016-01450/annual-update-o

f-the-hhs-poverty-guidelines

3. *NCCP | Head Start Family and Child Experiences Survey (FACES).* (2018).

Nccp.org. Retrieved 13 June 2018, from

http://www.nccp.org/publications/pub_1194.html

4. Webb. (2018). *Great Depression | Encyclopedia of Milwaukee. Emke.uwm.edu.*

Retrieved 18 November 2018, from https://emke.uwm.edu/entry/great-depression/

5. Medicaid for the Elderly, Blind, or Disabled. (2014). Wisconsin Department of

Health Services. Retrieved 9 December 2018, from

https://www.dhs.wisconsin.gov/medicaid/index.htm

6. *Rice University sociologists calculate caregivers' risk of living in poverty*. (2018).

News.rice.edu. Retrieved 1 December 2017, from

http://news.rice.edu/2004/08/16/rice-university-sociologists-calculate-caregivers-risk

-of-living-in-poverty/

7. *IRIS (Include, Respect, I Self-Direct). (2014). Wisconsin Department of Health

Services*. Retrieved 9 December 2018, from

https://www.dhs.wisconsin.gov/iris/index.htm

8. *Long Term Care Insurance Rates Cost Comparison from leading long term care

insurance companies. (2018). Aaltci.org*. Retrieved 9 December 2018, from

http://www.aaltci.org/long-term-care-insurance-rates/

9. *The Magnificent Mile - North Michigan Avenue, Chicago. (2018). The

Magnificent Mile*. Retrieved 9 December 2018, from

https://www.themagnificentmile.com/

10. *Obama's "war on religion". (2018). The Economist*. Retrieved 9 December

2018, from

https://www.economist.com/united-states/2012/02/11/obamas-war-on-religion

11. *State Reports Archive - Talk Poverty*. (2018). *Talk Poverty*. Retrieved 9 June 2018, from https://talkpoverty.org/state-year-report/

12. "North Side | March On Milwaukee - Libraries Digital Collection". 2018. *Uwm.Edu*. Accessed December 2 2018. https://uwm.edu/marchonmilwaukee/keyterms/north-side/

13. My mother was of what she called "bohemian" descent. My immediate family members are all caucasian.

14. "White Milwaukee Lied To Itself For Decades, And In 1967 The Truth Came Out". 2017. *Timeline*. Accessed December 2 2018. https://timeline.com/milwaukee-long-hot-summer-252057567975.

15. Germanson. (2019). *Workers' Movements | Encyclopedia of Milwaukee*. *Emke.uwm.edu*. Retrieved 9 January 2019, from https://emke.uwm.edu/entry/workers-movements/

16. "Medical Examiner: Half Of Infant Deaths In Milwaukee County In 2017 Related To Unsafe Sleep". 2018. *Jsonline*. Accessed December 3 2018.

17. "A Night Of Conflict, Chaos And Courage In Sherman Park". 2018. *Jsonline*. Accessed September 3 2018. https://www.jsonline.com/story/news/crime/2016/08/20/night-conflict-chaos-and-courage-sherman-park/88994022/.

18. "The 'Long, Hot Summer Of 1967'". 2017. *Theweek.Com*. Accessed September 3

2018. https://theweek.com/captured/712838/long-hot-summer-1967.

19. *Culture, Migration and the Rise of Nationalism | Inter Press Service*. (2018).

Ipsnews.net. Retrieved 10 December 2018, from

http://www.ipsnews.net/2018/11/culture-migration-rise-nationalism/

20. Williams, D. R. 2001. "Racial Residential Segregation: A Fundamental Cause

Of Racial Disparities In Health". *Public Health Reports* 116 (5): 404-416. SAGE

Publications. doi:10.1093/phr/116.5.404.

21. Massey, Douglas S., and Jonathan Tannen. 2015. "A Research Note On Trends

In Black Hypersegregation". *Demography* 52 (3): 1025-1034. Springer Nature.

doi:10.1007/s13524-015-0381-6.

22. When I contacted Douglas Massey to talk with him about his research on

hypersegregation, he referred me to the following books: *Great American City* by

Robert J. Sampson; *Stuck in Place* by Patrick Sharkey; and *Divergent Social Worlds*

by Ruth Peterson and Lauren Krivo. He said the books are good references because

they "have a lot of information about how segregation and the disparity in

neighborhood circumstances it produces affect human well-being, especially

children." All of the books look at the relationship between race and other divides.

23. Books that have focused on Milwaukee and its problems as an urban center include Kathleen Neils Conzen's *Immigrant Milwaukee, 1836-1860: Accommodation and Community in a Frontier City* (Cambridge: Harvard University Press, 1976) and Joe William Trotter, Jr.'s *Black Milwaukee: The Making of an Industrial Proletariat* (Urbana: University of Illinois Press, 1985); *Jonathon Coleman's controversial Long Way to Go: Black and White in America* (New York: Atlantic Monthly Press, 1997); and Matthew Desmond's *Evicted: Poverty and Profit in the American City* (Broadway Books, 2016)

24. "'Hypersegregated' U.S. Metros Are On The Decline". 2018. Citylab. Accessed April 2 2018.

https://www.citylab.com/equity/2015/05/america-has-half-as-many-hypersegregated-metros-as-it-did-in-1970/393743/.

25. *Brief History of Milwaukee - Children in Urban America.* (2017). *Marquette.edu.* Retrieved 1 April 2017, from

https://www.marquette.edu/cuap/milwpast.shtml

26. (2018). *Www4.uwm.edu.* Retrieved 24 November 2018, from

https://www4.uwm.edu/eti/Archives/RaciallyRestrictiveCovenants.pdf

27. *Greenfield, WI.* (2018). *Data USA.* Retrieved 24 November 2018, from

https://datausa.io/profile/geo/greenfield-wi/

28. *The Fair Housing Act*. (2015). *Justice.gov*. Retrieved 11 June 2017, from

https://www.justice.gov/crt/fair-housing-act-1

29. *ZIP Code 53214 Map, Housing Stats, More for West Allis, WI*. (2018).

Unitedstateszipcodes.org. Retrieved 9 December 2018, from

https://www.unitedstateszipcodes.org/53214/

30. staff, N. (2018). *Corner grocery stores: nutritional wasteland or opportunity for

improving communities?*. *National Consumers League*. Retrieved 9 December 2018,

from https://www.nclnet.org/corner_grocery_stores

31. (2018). *Arcgis.com*. Retrieved 9 December 2018, from

http://www.arcgis.com/apps/Compare/storytelling_compare/index.html?appid=5ff08

48aad224aeb93091df1c2fcd14f

32. "NCCP | Wisconsin: Demographics Of Poor Children". 2018. *Nccp.Org*.

Accessed December 2 2018.

http://www.nccp.org/profiles/state_profile.php?state=WI&id=7.

33. (2019). Tfah.org. Retrieved 30 January 2019, from

https://www.tfah.org/state-details/wisconsin/

34. "WI African American Eliminating Disparities Institute". 2018. *Black Health

Coalition Of Wisconsin Inc*. Accessed December 4 2018.

http://www.bhcw.org/wi--african-american-eliminating-disparities-institute.html.

35. *Fewer Wisconsin children have health insurance than they did last year - The Daily Cardinal*. (2018). *The Daily Cardinal*. Retrieved 10 December 2018, from http://www.dailycardinal.com/article/2018/11/fewer-wisconsin-children-have-health-insurance-than-they-did-last-year

36. *Beyond Health Care: The Role of Social Determinants in Promoting Health and Health Equity*. (2018). *The Henry J. Kaiser Family Foundation*. Retrieved 6 December 2018, from https://www.kff.org/disparities-policy/issue-brief/beyond-health-care-the-role-of-social-determinants-in-promoting-health-and-health-equity/

37. *Milwaukee infant mortality rates heading in wrong direction*. (2019). *Archive.jsonline.com*. Retrieved 10 January 2019, from http://archive.jsonline.com/news/milwaukee/milwaukee-infant-mortality-rates-heading-in-wrong-direction-b99282687z1-261616401.html/

38. *Wisconsin's Infant Mortality For African-Americans Highest In Nation*. (2018). *Wisconsin Public Radio*. Retrieved 10 January 2019, from https://www.wpr.org/wisconsins-infant-mortality-african-americans-highest-nation

39. (2018). *Whitehouse.gov*. Retrieved 6 December 2018, from https://www.whitehouse.gov/wp-content/uploads/2018/07/Expanding-Work-Requirements-in-Non-Cash-Welfare-Programs.pdf

40. *Cuts to Prevention and Public Health Fund Puts CDC Programs at Risk*. (2018).

The Scientist Magazine. Retrieved 6 December 2018, from

https://www.the-scientist.com/daily-news/cuts-to-prevention-and-public-health-fund-

puts-cdc-programs-at-risk-30298

41. *http://time.com*. (2018). *Money*. Retrieved 10 December 2018, from

http://time.com/money/5269269/the-trump-administration-wants-to-cancel-7-billion-

from-a-childrens-health-insurance-program/

42. *Darienne Driver is leaving MPS for position at United Way in Michigan*. (2018).

jsonline. Retrieved 4 December 2018, from

https://www.jsonline.com/story/news/education/2018/04/03/darienne-driver-leaving-

mps-position-united-way-michigan/482140002/

43. *Darienne Driver is leaving MPS for position at United Way in Michigan*. (2018).

jsonline. Retrieved 12 May 2018, from

https://www.jsonline.com/story/news/education/2018/04/03/darienne-driver-leaving-

mps-position-united-way-michigan/482140002/

44. *Scott Walker's path to power | Journal Sentinel - jsonline.com*. (2019).

Projects.jsonline.com. Retrieved 9 January 2019, from

https://projects.jsonline.com/news/2016/11/27/scott-walkers-path-to-power.html

45. *SPEECH: State of Education.* (2018). *Wisconsin Department of Public Instruction.* Retrieved 5 November 2018, from

https://dpi.wi.gov/news/releases/2018/speech-state-education

46. Author's note: This comment reminds me of the statement made in a class by Ivy Wilson, Northwestern University instructor on comparative literatures of the black diaspora.

47. *Walker: Wis. won't set up exchange.* (2018). *Thecurrent.org.* Retrieved 4 December 2018, from

https://www.thecurrent.org/feature/2012/11/16/politics/walker-wisconsin-health-exchange

48. *Walker rejects full Medicaid expansion.* (2018). *Archive.jsonline.com.* Retrieved 4 December 2018, from

http://archive.jsonline.com/news/statepolitics/gov-scott-walkers-badgercare-plan-would-insure-224000-more-people-ij8p25s-191079601.html/

49. *HEALTHCARE - Tony Evers for Wisconsin.* (2018). *Tony Evers for Wisconsin.* Retrieved 6 December 2018, from https://tonyevers.com/plan/healthcare/

50. (2018). *Jsonline.com.* Retrieved 4 December 2018, from

https://www.jsonline.com/story/news/politics/elections/2018/12/04/republicans-vote-tuesday-curbing-powers-tony-evers-limiting-early-voting/2198624002/

51. *Wisconsin Gov.-Elect Tony Evers Will Ask Scott Walker To Veto GOP Power Grab*. (2018). *HuffPost*. Retrieved 6 December 2018, from

https://www.huffingtonpost.com/entry/tony-evers-walker-republican-power-grab_us_5c087993e4b0844cda4fbb25

52. *The Latest: Evers to appeal to Walker to veto GOP power play*. (2018). *AP NEWS*. Retrieved 6 December 2018, from

https://www.apnews.com/dbded03c16ce4c3c8609d01b403e57d9

53. *Evers asks Walker to veto lame-duck bills*. (2018). *WSAU*. Retrieved 6 December 2018, from

https://wsau.com/news/articles/2018/dec/06/evers-asks-walker-to-veto-lame-duck-bills/

54. When my mother's brother, Harry, died from TB it was a disease of shame. My mother talks about how her brother, only 17 at the time, was kept upstairs. He was a young artist and filled the top floor with sketches of the Green Bay Packers in action. Even he didn't know what was wrong with him until his mother, my grandmother, was told by the doctor in front of him that he should be moved to a sanitarium. My mother said that after he died my grandmother took all of his things out of the house to let the sunshine "disinfect" his belongings, including his bed. Those things were then passed along to my mother, but she survived.

55. *NVSS - United States Small-Area Life Expectancy Estimates Project.* (2018).

Cdc.gov. Retrieved 2 December 2018, from

https://www.cdc.gov/nchs/nvss/usaleep/usaleep.html

56. *Healthiest Wisconsin 2020 Baseline and Health Disparities Report.* (2014).

Wisconsin Department of Health Services. Retrieved 10 December 2018, from

https://www.dhs.wisconsin.gov/hw2020/baseline.htm

57. "Could Where You Are Born Influence How Long You Live?". 2018. *RWJF.*

Accessed June 13 2018.

https://www.rwjf.org/en/library/interactives/whereyouliveaffectshowlongyoulive.htm

l

58. Kersten, E., Adler, N., Gottlieb, L., Jutte, D., Robinson, S., Roundfield, K., &

LeWinn, K. (2017). Neighborhood Child Opportunity and Individual-Level Pediatric

Acute Care Use and Diagnoses. *Pediatrics, 141*(5), e20172309.

doi:10.1542/peds.2017-2309

59. (2018). *Fox6now.com.* Retrieved 27 November 2018, from

https://fox6now.com/2018/11/27/neighbors-concerned-over-planned-changes-at-park

lawn-ymca-these-kids-this-is-all-theyve-got/

60. Some reports indicate Silver Sneakers programs pay traditional health clubs a

fee of around $30 for each member per month. Writer, D. (2018). *Local fitness centers benefit from 'Silver Sneakers' amid competition for members. The State*

Journal. Retrieved 8 December 2018, from

https://www.sj-r.com/article/20140307/News/140309401

61. (2018). *City.milwaukee.gov.* Retrieved 28 November 2018, from

https://city.milwaukee.gov/ImageLibrary/Groups/ccCouncil/News/2018/District07/1

1_28YMCAstatement.pdf

62. *Walker: Wis. won't set up health exchange.* (2018). *Thecurrent.org.* Retrieved 4

December 2018, from

https://www.thecurrent.org/feature/2012/11/16/politics/walker-wisconsin-health-exc

hange

63. *Walker rejects full Medicaid expansion.* (2018). *Archive.jsonline.com.* Retrieved

4 December 2018, from

http://archive.jsonline.com/news/statepolitics/gov-scott-walkers-badgercare-plan-wo

uld-insure-224000-more-people-ij8p25s-191079601.html/

64. *HEALTHCARE - Tony Evers for Wisconsin.* (2018). *Tony Evers for Wisconsin.*

Retrieved 6 December 2018, from https://tonyevers.com/plan/healthcare/

65. Members, G. (2018). *Governor-Elect Tony Evers and Lt. Gov.-Elect Mandela*

Barnes Announce Diverse Health Advisory Board Members. Our Lives. Retrieved 10

December 2018,

http://ourlivesmadison.com/governor-elect-tony-evers-and-lt-gov-elect-mandela-barnes-announce-diverse-health-advisory-board-members/

66. (2018). *Files.kff.org*. Retrieved 10 December 2018, from

http://files.kff.org/attachment/fact-sheet-medicaid-state-WI

67. Rovner, J. (2018). *A Texas Lawsuit Being Heard This Week Could Mean Life Or Death For The ACA. Kaiser Health News*. Retrieved 10 December 2018, from

https://khn.org/news/democratic-gop-attorneys-general-square-off-in-texas-showdown-over-health-law/

68. *Universal Declaration of Human Rights*. (2015). *Un.org*. Retrieved 9 December 2018, from http://www.un.org/en/universal-declaration-uman-rights/

69. Communities in Action. (2017). doi:10.17226/24624

70. *Confronting Asian-American Stereotypes*. (2018). *Nytimes.com*. Retrieved 9 December 2018, from

https://www.nytimes.com/2018/06/23/us/confronting-asian-american-stereotypes.html

71. America Becoming. (2001). doi:10.17226/9599

72. *Get 2019 health coverage. Health Insurance Marketplace* . (2018). *HealthCare.gov*. Retrieved 9 December 2018, from https://www.healthcare.gov/

73. Media reports indicate only 62,000 people Wisconsinites signed up for insurance

through the Affordable Care Act in 2018, compared to 78,000 the previous year.

Wisconsin health care signups decline in 2018. (2018). *WISC.* Retrieved 10

December 2018, from

https://www.channel3000.com/news/wisconsin-health-care-signups-decline-in-2018-

1/902721952

74. (2018). *Icrc.org.* Retrieved 18 March 2018, from

https://www.icrc.org/eng/assets/files/other/irrc_858_krafess.pdf

75. *Various Physicians Oaths.* (2018). *Aapsonline.org.* Retrieved 18 March 2018,

from http://www.aapsonline.org/ethics/oaths.htm

76. *WI African American Eliminating Disparities Institute.* (2018). *Black Health

Coalition of WIsconsin Inc.* Retrieved 5 December 2018, from

http://www.bhcw.org/wi--african-american-eliminating-disparities-institute.html

77. *Fewer Wisconsin children have health insurance than they did last year - The

Daily Cardinal.* (2018). *The Daily Cardinal.* Retrieved 10 December 2018, from

http://www.dailycardinal.com/article/2018/11/fewer-wisconsin-children-have-health-

insurance-than-they-did-last-year

78. (2018). *Whitehouse.gov*. Retrieved 6 December 2018, from

https://www.whitehouse.gov/wp-content/uploads/2018/07/Expanding-Work-Require

ments-in-Non-Cash-Welfare-Programs.pdf

79. *Cuts to Prevention and Public Health Fund Puts CDC Programs at Risk*. (2018).

The Scientist Magazine. Retrieved 6 December 2018, from

https://www.the-scientist.com/daily-news/cuts-to-prevention-and-public-health-fund-

puts-cdc-programs-at-risk-30298

80. *http://time.com*. (2018). *Money*. Retrieved 10 December 2018, from

http://time.com/money/5269269/the-trump-administration-wants-to-cancel-7-billion-

from-a-childrens-health-insurance-program/

81. *History & Origins of HCZ | Harlem Children's Zone*. (2018). *Harlem Children's*

Zone. Retrieved 10 December 2018, from https://hcz.org/about-us/history/

82. *Opportunity Zones About - Economic Innovation Group*. (2018). *Economic*

Innovation Group. Retrieved 10 December 2018, from

https://eig.org/opportunityzones/about

83. (2018). *Whitehouse.gov*. Retrieved 10 December 2018, from

https://www.whitehouse.gov/wp-content/uploads/2018/02/WH_CuttingTaxesForAm

ericanWorkers_Feb2018.pdf

AUTHOR BIO

Christine Marie Nielsen is an award-winning journalist, inventor and entrepreneur. She spent close to 20 years covering financial markets, working as a staff writer for Dow Jones News Service and Knight-Ridder Financial. She has also served as a contributing intercultural editor to writers in over 75 countries for media outlets including the *The Christian Science Monitor* and *Living Earth Television.*

In 2020, Nielsen's LLC, Geodialog Media, was one of 27 companies chosen to participate in the SPARC cohort program from Scale Up Milwaukee. Scale Up Milwaukee has the stated purpose of generating inclusive prosperity. Nielsen was the first person in her family to receive a college degree (BA in Journalism with a Minor in English from Marquette University and later an MA in Creative Writing from Northwestern University). She was also the first person in her family to have her own business.

Nielsen invented Dialog Journalism® in 2011 and stated its aim to the USPTO as a solution-focused dissemination of news that integrates traditional international editorial content and an online social media forum in an effort to resolve global issues. She was also one of the first women involved in the tech journo space, designing a platform and news delivery system for Dialog Journalism® about the

same time.

-END-